THE LADY AND HER PURSE

BREAKING LIMITING MINDSETS FINANCIALLY TO RISE ABOVE SITUATIONS

OLAMITOYOSI BABATUNDE

THE LADY AND HER PURSE

WRITTEN BY
OLAMITOYOSI BABATUNDE
olammybabs@gmail.com

COPYRIGHT (C) 2023

ALL RIGHTS RESERVED. No part of this book may be reproduced or transmitted in any form or by any means, electronic or mechanical, including photocopying, recording, or by any information storage and retrieval system, without written permission from the author or publisher.

Published by:
COMMUNE WRITERS INT'L
www.communewriters.com
+234 8139 260 389
6, Amusa Street, Agodo-Egbe, Lagos.

Published in the Federal Republic of Nigeria

PRAISE FOR THE LADY AND HER PURSE

I give this book a 5 star because of the story telling approach the author used to convey the message of financial literacy. The book has given me a structure or should I say a guide on how I can begin to teach my daughter about her purse. My purse is my enabler and God's will for me is to have my purse full.

Abisayo Adewole

I thoroughly enjoyed reading this book. The language was simple and easy to understand. The examples the author shared while taking time to list the people she looked up to was very valuable.

Evelyn Ekarika

This book is engaging and coming from the author's personal experiences, it is authentic and I find it doable. I will recommend it not only for women but men as well. The issue of finance cuts across gender and age. Although the book speaks more to women but men has a lot to learn in backing the women in their lives up and encouraging them to spread their wings and overcome their fears about generating income.

Oluremi Oyinlola

CONTENTS

Dedication   *i*

Acknowledgement   *ii*

Foreword   *iv*

Chapter 1
A Little Backstory   1

Chapter 2
Fast Forward   8

Chapter 3
Why does a Lady need her purse?   18

Chapter 4
Nuggets for the purse   23

Conclusion   37

About the Author   41

DEDICATION

This book is dedicated to every lady out there who desires to do better with her finances.

I see you and I hear you.

ACKNOWLEDGEMENT

I am sincerely grateful to everyone who has believed in me. I am grateful to my parents, siblings for always believing in me and giving me the space to be me.

Thank you to my Pastors for always being there. Thank you, Dr. Titi for reminding me that the world needs to benefit from my gift.

I am thankful for my husband, Olorunfemi and my children for their support and faith in me. I am thankful to my mentees and coaching clients who never get tired of my propensity to push them in all areas of life.

Mrs. Gbonjubola Sanni, thank you for being a mentor and a sister from the days of The Financial Diva. Thank you for agreeing to write the Foreword at such a personally trying time.

Mrs. Blessing Enekwechi – thank you for sharing your thoughts and reading through for a final edit.

Thank you, Mrs. Kemisola (Ajetunmobi) Ilori for giving me the challenge to write this particular piece.

I am grateful to everyone who read the draft and shared their candid feedback.

I am thankful for you, dear reader, yes, YOU! We are on a journey together.

FOREWORD

We never can tell the effect our growing up years have on us till we are grown and able to look back in retrospect to see how things stringed together to get us where we are.

One thing that's very important to note like Olamitoyosi mentioned in this book is that you may not be able to change your start point but you can change your destination.

The topic of "women and money" continue to be an interesting one and it's important that women take the bull by the horns so they can create the kind of life they want. Not only will that happen but you will create liberation for the generation to come as children and the younger generation are more influenced than we think by our actions or inactions.

Every chapter of this book, starting from the backstory to the conclusion, is loaded with tips and ideas that will stimulate you to understand that your financial journey has an effect on others as well as it does on you.

It's time for you to give your financial journey the push required to enable you to achieve the impact and influence you were created to have. Don't keep this to yourself, pick copies for others who need to read this and let's make the world better because we are here.

To your financial and all-round success,

Gbonjubola Sanni

#1
A LITTLE BACKSTORY

My name is Olamitoyosi Babatunde. I was born and bred in Ibadan Oyo state. As the last born, I attended the same schools as my siblings and seemed to grow in their shadows sometimes but often found myself trying to prove that I was different and me.

My dad was a civil engineer while my mum was a teacher in the state's teaching service. We were well off financially – that much my siblings and I believed until one day when a schoolmate's dad told me my dad was rich. I was taken aback and replied that I didn't know, I just knew we were doing okay. As I grew older, I often heard comments from people around to suggest that we were more than comfortable. I found out that my parents were quite generous, helping families who needed help financially and that they also had a large heart. I think we all inherited these traits from them.

A time, however, came when my dad's business suffered a fatal blow from which it never recovered. My mum was close to retirement then, but her job still helped considerably. The financial challenges we had and the lack that we sometimes experienced as a result of that helped shape us somehow. Interestingly, our parents had never shown any lavish display of wealth; instead, we were brought up to be frugal; so it was easier for them when things changed. We never complained. We all pitched in to help in any way we could.

As the last born, I was the only one left in secondary school then. At a certain period, it became very difficult to give me transport fare to school while I was in SS1. My school was far from our home and to this day, I am thankful that till I finished, no one ever thought of or mentioned changing my school. There were so many things I took away from finishing at that same school, St. Anne's School, Molete, Ibadan in South West Nigeria. To raise transport fares to school, I would make chin chin (*a fried snack made from pastry and cut into bite sizes*) to sell to my classmates. I would take out the capital every day and keep my profits as the transport fare to school the next day. Then I would buy the things I needed and make the next day's batch.

One day, I thought of adding the profits to the capital to make more but I dared not, so I only added a little more. It was amazing, but aside from my breakfast, I wouldn't eat anything else till I got home at that time which was usually in the evening. Sometimes, I would walk part of the distance home to save money, especially if we needed to pay for something at school because I hated to bother my parents. That period it seemed laid a foundation for the strong and independent woman that I am today. One day, my mum was in the area and visited my school to see her colleagues. While there, she observed some students being punished for not making a particular payment for a project in one subject. She pulled me aside and whispered in hushed tones.

"You have not paid for that project too," She whispered.

Confidently, I replied, "I have ma."

"When and where did you get the money from?" She queried.

I told her the money had come from some savings I made by walking home from my extra mural classes in the evening which was situated halfway between school and home. I could tell that she was not just relieved, she felt grateful and added in a teary voice that I shouldn't walk so much.

Too bad, I had begun to enjoy the cool evening breeze and chats with my friends who would all stop some distance before me but the rest of the walk home was when I started my conversations with God. I would tell him about my dreams and sometimes, just talk to Him. That was up till 1999.

Between 1999 and 2005, I gained admission into the university at the same time as my immediate elder sister and through the family financial challenges and the seemingly ever-present lack we rose and excelled in our studies and walk with God.

We walked when it was necessary and boarded vehicles when it was possible. I remember one particular incident when I went to Glory Tabernacle

Church, Bodija to watch one of Mount Zion's newest films. I stayed in Idia Hall at the University of Ibadan at that time. I trekked from Idia Hall to UI Main Gate and then boarded a bus to the venue at Bodija. After watching the film, I trekked back to UI main gate and then boarded a bus back to Idia Hall, a distance of 3.1km.

All these experiences taught me to be frugal such that when I went in for my Masters' degree programme at the same University of Ibadan, I kept a careful record of all expenses down to the photocopies we made, food I ate or even the water I drank. I was that intentional about my finances. But at that time, all I understood was savings and being frugal. Even though our dad had introduced us to stocks – something that proved helpful to us as a family at several points, I didn't think I could invest in anything until after I was well-established financially.

WORKBOOK ACTIVITIES

Reflect on your personal experiences.

- What were my early experiences with money?

_____

_____

_____

_____

_____

_____

- What did they teach me?

_____

_____

_____

_____

_____

_____

#2
FAST FORWARD

I got married in 2009 but we didn't have our first child until 2011. We were both growing our careers and things were moving steadily though sometimes tough. Paying our son's fees was a major project yet we would pay it in instalments. Things got better when we had our second child but I still had some concerns.

Then in 2014, I had a brainwave.

Many mothers, I inclusive pray for our children to be great. We want them to be renowned for something great; sometimes, we pray for them to stand tall in the world. But the way things were going, it didn't seem that our children would be able to attend Harvard, Yale or stand with the children of wealthy people like Alhaji Aliko Dangote, Femi Otedola or Folorunso Alakija.

It was brutal truth but I needed to be sincere with myself and face the reality. I began to talk to God about it. Now, I said talk because that is what I do many times when I feel overwhelmed, I have conversations with God like a friend or someone I can see physically. During one of these conversations, I felt an impression to do a little research on rich young people under thirty – five (35) years. In hindsight, I realised I should have taken notes. Despite this error, the lessons I took away from the research, I wear close like a shield.

Here is my major discovery:

There are three classes of rich people.

Group 1: Those who inherit wealth. This wealth in most cases came from the parents or close relatives. Some of these young people were spoiled and only managed to hold on to their wealth. A rare few bought into the vision that generated the family wealth and multiplied the wealth in the process.

Group 2: This group did not come from wealthy families. Their families were business owners and entrepreneurs who ran profitable businesses and managed to make their families comfortable. As a result, the young people from these groups are financially intelligent and business savvy. They, then use these skills to multiply wealth thus becoming wealthier than their parents. They make it into the top echelon of the world of finance.

Group 3: The final group of rich young people were from poor families. As they grew older, they were challenged by their background and worked hard, learning all they could to move from their financial status into one of wealth.

These lessons were a defining moment for me. As I mentioned in the beginning, my family could be described as a middle-income family. We were comfortable, and travelling out of Nigeria was something we did when I was a baby. My mum finally returned to Nigeria when I was five years old and somehow at the back of my mind, I had this vague thought that one day, I would be able to travel out of Nigeria again, even send my children to higher institutions there. At the moment of the research, my husband was earning a good income and so was I, relatively. Paradoxically, I could not be said to come from a poor background (group 3) or a rich one (group 1). That left me with group 2 but I did not qualify either. My mum was a retired teacher from government service and my dad's business did not fare well for many years. My husband and I were in paid employment so the business family (group 2) was certainly not us too.

What was my issue? I wanted my children to be successful and wealthy. One key factor that I picked from the three groups was that these people learnt the principles of wealth and multiplication. They were financially intelligent. So, I decided that I would teach my children to be financially informed.

There was a problem with this decision. I had just a little knowledge of financial management. What I had learnt about balance sheets from my Nigeria Institute of Management (NIM) and about shares was not enough to teach my children, not to mention that they were not age-appropriate for my three-year-old son and his one-year-old sister at the time. **How do you give what you don't have?**

I realised that I would have to gain sound financial knowledge and find age-appropriate

materials to teach my children about money. That was the start of a whole new world for me. I read everything I could find online when I could. I followed anyone who seemed to have something to offer where money was concerned. Parenting was something I already had a passion for and also because of my job as a teacher and school leader, I followed Praise Fowowe on Twitter to learn about sex education amongst other things. Sometimes, he would retweet tweets by some people. That way, I followed Tosin Praise Fowowe, an expert on Family finance. I followed Tade Cash, long before I knew who he was or met him in person. I followed Gbonjubola Sanni who is a financial expert on women's and children's finance. My approach was once I read your post and it resonated with me, I would go to your handle or page and click follow. Once, I stopped following someone because I wasn't getting any value from his page again.

I met Tomiwa Sangonuga at work one day while he was on a business transaction and he introduced some books for sale to parents of children in our school – the books were financial literacy books for children and teenagers. The one for children was for children aged three years and above. I practically jumped at the books. Interestingly, two of the three books were written by Gbonjubola Sanni and a friend. I was to later become better acquainted with Gbonjubola Sanni in my quest and eventually, have her as a financial mentor.

It became glaring at some point on my financial journey that even though I had set out to teach my children how to be rich in a godly way, it wasn't too late for me to become work on my finances too. It was a real eye-opener for me and I embraced it with open arms.

I began to learn more and not limit my learning to children's finance anymore. I began to follow people like Aliko Dangote, Folorunsho Alakija, Richard Branson, Temi Ashabi – Ajibewa, Arese Ugwu, Nimi Akinkugbe, Bill and Melinda Gates, Strive Masiyiwa, Dave Ramsey and several others.

It was from Tade Cash I learnt that God expects us to have a minimum of four streams of income. Some people might disagree but not Gbonjubola Sanni who motivates us to have that as a minimum as well. I am still on this journey but my children are certainly better because I teach as I learn. They have not fully comprehended some principles but our journey is beautiful and it is not yet over.

WORKBOOK ACTIVITIES

Reflect on your personal experiences.

- Where am I in my finances?

_____

_____

_____

_____

- Is it where I want to be?

_____

_____

_____

- Am I content to be at this level for now?

_____

_____

_____

- Where do I want to be in my finances?

  _____

  _____

  _____

  _____

  _____

- What steps do I need to take?

  _____

  _____

  _____

  _____

  _____

#3
WHY DOES A LADY NEED HER PURSE?

Purse as used in this book refers to earnings. The English dictionary defines a purse as "a small pouch of leather or plastic used for carrying money, typically by a woman."

1. It commands respect.

In the last couple of years, I have read disheartening accounts of women who are down on their luck and maltreated by family or other people because they depend on these people for survival. Let that same woman find her feet and have some substantial money in her bank account or a booming business, the same people suddenly become nice.

2. **It gives you a voice.**

If one takes a look at the statistics of women who command some wealth or reputable organization, people want to hear the woman. They seek her opinion. Having your own wealth can give you the voice you seek.

3. **It sharpens your problem-solving and thinking reflexes.**

Making money is one thing, managing and multiplying the money is another. Managing and multiplying money requires good problem-solving skills and the ability to think on your feet. When you manage for someone else, the level of reflex is not usually as high as managing and multiplying your own.

4. **It is an enabler.**

Money is an enabler. It empowers, it makes you achieve faster and better than when there is none. "The more your money works for you, the less you have to work for money." - *Idowu Koyenikan*

5. It positions you to participate.

In the Holy Scriptures, there is a story of a poor wise man whose wisdom saved a city. He was soon forgotten. Why? He was poor. The wealthy also employs the knowledgeable so it is not enough to have the technical know-how, it is important to get a seat at the table of wealth because it brings recognition.

6. It is the will of the Father.

The Holy Bible teaches that it is God who gives us the power to make wealth. In another place, it explains how God is willing to give us all we need and excess so that we can be comfortable and also give to 'every good work."

In some cultures, there are stereotypes about money that need to be addressed on a personal level otherwise they become strongholds in the mind of the individual. Strongholds that are so familiar the person might not realise how inhibiting they are. The following workbook activities would help you examine your money thoughts.

WORKBOOK ACTIVITIES

Note: Dear reader, you deserve to be comfortable. You deserve to be wealthy too. Now ask yourself:

- What are my thoughts about money?

_____
_____
_____
_____
_____
_____

#4
NUGGETS FOR THE PURSE

I have taken a lot away from this journey and having shared my background to this learning, here is my summary.

1. Riches belong to everyone.

Even though riches belong to everyone, it is only those who desire them and work towards them lay hold on them.

Many of us hope to be rich. Hope is good but it doesn't bring dreams to pass. It only keeps dreams alive. It is not enough to hope, you have to actively work for your goals. Hope doesn't put money in the pocket, it doesn't set goals or achieve targets. HOPE IS

NOT ENOUGH. As powerful as faith is, the Bible says in James 2: 14 that faith without works is dead. How much so, hope?

2. It is not a sin to be rich.

This applies more to Christians. Many of us were raised to think it is a sin to be rich. We even quote the scripture wrongly to say 'money is the root of all evil'. Meanwhile, what the Bible says in 1 Timothy 6: 10 is – '*The **love** of money is the root of all evil. Some people eager for money have wandered from the faith and pierced themselves with many griefs*' (NIV). God has given us the power to make wealth. Would He do that if it was a sin to be rich?

Sometimes, we see it as an affront when someone makes a statement like, 'I am rich' or 'I want to be rich. As long as we do not think our wealth is by our power, strength, wisdom or intelligence, we are not walking in sin. The moment we place our riches or the search for them above our search for God, then we are outside the will of God and headed for disaster in the long run.

3. Money flows.

It comes from the same root word as the **current** which describes something that flows like water or power. According to Merriam-Webster's online dictionary, the **Latin word** *currere*, meaning "to run," and its form *'cursus'* give us the **roots** *'curr'* and *curs*. Words from the Latin 'currere' have something to do with running or flowing water such as Undercurrent, Countercurrent, Current Account, and Current Assets to mention a few.

Trying to dam (store) money keeps it at the same level. You need to make money liquid, and keep it flowing to multiply and grow money. In the same light, you have to tell money where to go. Direct it where you want or need it to go otherwise it would flow away. If you earn money before you plan for it, chances are that you would not be able to account for how you spent a good portion of it.

Now imagine what happens when you earn money without any plan for it. It's a financial disaster and a proponent for living in penury. This is where budgeting comes in. Having a budget helps to determine where your money flows to. Even when something unexpected comes up, proper budgeting would help you to accommodate it or determine where it comes in.

4. Mothers have the power to change the course of generations.

I was determined to give my children a platform to stand tall anywhere in the world. I wanted to give them that footing to converse and be recognised for their rights, to make landmark achievements. Though they are still young and we are not there yet, we are certainly on our way there. It didn't matter whether their dad and I come from wealthy families, business families or not, I decided to change where we were and where our children would be.

To be candid, anyone can make a change and rewrite history as long as the person puts in the hard work and stays focused; not forgetting the place of the God-factor.

5. You may not be able to change your start point but you can change your destination.

Yes, you were born into that situation but remaining there is your choice. There are so many stories of people with humble beginnings who changed the course of their lives with a single decision. So whether, you were born with a silver spoon, a wooden spoon or no spoon at all, get up and get to work so you end up giving silver spoons to many who have no one to give them silver spoons.

Now, I am not just trying to change the course of my loved ones financially, my husband and I have goals and the vision to help others who have no one. Already, we had done that with what we had in the past but that is just the tip of the iceberg.

Make up your mind to end well and leave a legacy for your children's children. A wise man once said that one needs to leave at least a house for each child, understanding that a house is an asset and not a liability. Leaving cars and clothes is not bad but they are liabilities, not assets; it takes money to maintain them.

6. Every woman deserves her own.

Today's economic world requires that the members of a family work together. There are uncertainties in life so depending on only one partner's income might not be the smartest decision. Moreover, there was a time when I was in between jobs and my husband's salary was all we had. Thankfully, we did not have children then. It was quite tough.

One day, my husband suggested that I made pastries for his colleagues daily as a way of raising some cash on my own. I found out that I felt more confident with the little cash I made as a profit every day. I was also able to buy small household items and food items without waiting for my husband to get back home or give me money.

In addition to this, I had observed one day that I was losing my edge as a person. Earning money of my own again began to sharpen the 'dull edges' and by the time I started working in paid employment again, my confidence was back and my senses fully alert. I no longer felt as dull.

What is the point here? Have your own. Don't turn your spouse into an ATM. Give some relief by contributing financially to the family. There are things that I sort out on my own without my husband having to worry his head about them. Permit me to add that I was raised that way. Our Dad travelled often because of his work but things were sorted as the needs arose. My mum, even though she was a teacher and teachers were not well paid in those days, would attend to every need as they came up.

Another reason is exemplified in this scenario. At a time, I was driving a Honda and it was a birthday gift from my husband years before. Every day, I would give people a ride either to or from work. One day, I realised that my car was overloaded and it was hurting the car. I wasn't happy about it and began to pray for intervention. However, I couldn't even hope or dream of a new and bigger car because that one was a gift after all and the financial situation at home didn't leave room for anything extra. Not to mention, I simply couldn't afford a car. Not on the average teacher's salary, head or not.

But at the end of 2017, while setting goals for 2018, I set a goal to buy a bigger vehicle, I had specific details I wanted to meet as well. What changed for me barely a few months into the challenge? I added a new stream of income by registering as a Consultant with Oriflame Nigeria towards the end of the year. In doing so, I had a goal of what monthly income I was going to earn. So while setting goals for the year, I was able to project based on this new income target which spurred me to set a realistic goal of buying myself a car. It was a defining goal. I call it defining because there was first a shift in my thinking. I used to think I couldn't change my car until my husband decided to do so. Judging by the many responsibilities we had and the teething period of young businesses, I knew a new car was something I couldn't bring myself to hope for, let alone ask for. But now, I have the courage not to just make it a goal, I have spoken with car dealers and given them my specifications. Of course, both dealers wanted to offer me something else, even cute but I knew why I wanted another car, I wasn't dissatisfied with my present car, it was simply no longer meeting my need.

This power helped me to remain firm in my requests to both of them. Above all, the confidence I had told me that I had changed my thinking and money attitude. I may not have that particular car at the moment but my outlook has changed just like my self-worth and net worth.

I did change my car eventually after some time and even though it was with my husband's support, it felt good to price different vehicles and discuss specifications. It was another shift. A different dimension of thinking.

7. God has given us the power to make wealth, male, female, old or young.

Examples include (in ancient times), the Queen of Sheba or Lydia, the seller of purple (royal) clothes, or contemporary times, Liliane Bettencourt, Folorunsho Alakija, Melinda Gates, Mo Abudu and so many more, wealth does not answer to gender or age but to principles. He will bless as many as seek him and work with His principles for multiplying wealth.

8. If you want to be rich, you must have income from different industries.

I learnt this when I lamented to God in another conversation about being hard up even though I had monies with people who were yet to pay for services rendered. As I finished talking, He pointed out the fact that all my monies were in the same industry and this industry was at an all-time low being the end of one school year transitioning into the next school year. So even though none of these people denied owing me some money, none was able to pay at the time.

That day, I received illumination that to be rich or wealthy, you need to have investments or income drivers from different industries. That way, you find that you hardly run out of income. It means that when one source is slow (bearish like the stock market would say) another source might be moving along nicely or even fast (bullish).

9. Understand basic financial principles.

Understand basic financial principles such as budgeting, assets and liabilities, income and expenditure – basic cash flow.

Learn basic financial skills. You should have a budget for any income you are expecting. Even windfall must have a budget. This means that by the time money comes into your hand, you can channel it in the right direction.

In layman's language, an asset generates income – that is, it brings in money for you while a liability makes you spend money. Always have more assets than liabilities. If you must have a liability, create an asset to feed that liability. For instance, when our son was to start playing the keyboard, we had to look for a source of income with which to pay his music tuition so it didn't eat into our existing income. That is an example of creating an asset to feed a liability. Liabilities are not bad things, it is poor management that can make them appear as drains.

WORKBOOK ACTIVITIES

Reflect on your personal experience.

- What are my money habits? How do I behave with money - "let's spend whatever is available for the now or ...?"

_____

_____

_____

_____

_____

_____

FINALLY

In conclusion, have a structure and stick with it as long as it works. You may refine it but don't ever get rid of a winning team, especially when you seem to have arrived.

Don't splurge and spend carelessly when you have more income, rather invest it. Saving is old school, investment is the new school. It is good to save but it is better to invest.

Investment is sending your money on an errand to bring in some more. There are so many investment portfolios such as money markets, Forex trading, mutual funds and Insurance, and Bonds amongst others. Find a viable one around you, walk into your bank and ask for investment advice.

Riches are a gift from God, first to serve Him and then to bless humankind. Don't deny other people the blessing you could be to them by hiding away in lack.

It is God that gives the power to make wealth. In the beginning, He said, 'be fruitful and multiply and have dominion...' if you don't experience all of these, it is because you choose not to do so. Choose to be rich and disciplined. Choose to enjoy the best of God and the blessing that He has so freely declared. Stop limiting yourself. Break away from those thoughts that tell you "you can't." Break free from the limits in your mind. God told Abraham, "in blessing, I will bless you." In colloquial terms, he promised Abraham to back him up till his fears will cease. You have the same ability, don't sit on your hands, and don't hide that one coin, trade with it till it is multiplied many times.

Break free from all that holds you and go beyond the limits!

I celebrate you.

WORKBOOK ACTIVITIES

Reflect on your personal experiences.

_____
_____
_____
_____
_____
_____
_____
_____
_____
_____

FURTHER READING

- A-Z of Finance by Nimi Akinkugbe
- Think and Grow Rich by Napoleon Hill
- The Secret by Rhonda Byrne
- The Smart Money Woman by Arese Ugwu
- The Financial Diva Group by Gbonjubola Sanni
- ABC of Financial Intelligence for Kids by Gbonjubola Sanni and Adeolu Akinyemi

ABOUT THE AUTHOR

Olamitoyosi is a mother of two wonderful children and is happily married to Olorunfemi Babatunde. Having been married for fourteen years and counting, she has learnt valuable life lessons on family finances and the role a woman plays to ensure growth and harmony. With the lesson shared in this book, she has been able to increase her financial worth by starting from her mind.

Olamitoyosi is a school head and brings her years of experience to bear in people development and working with families. She lives in Lagos, Nigeria with her family.

www.ingramcontent.com/pod-product-compliance
Lightning Source LLC
Chambersburg PA
CBHW031534210526
45464CB00013B/1258